# CULTURE
## TRANSFORMATION
### PURPOSE, PASSION, PATH

The Principles for Success

## BY PHIL GELDART

EAGLE'S
FLIGHT™

Copyright © 2014
Eagle's Flight, Creative Training Excellence Inc.
ISBN 978-0-9939360-2-9

"As the mountains surround Jerusalem, so the Lord surrounds His people,
from this time forth and forevermore."
Psalms 125:2

# To the Reader

Culture Transformation is clearly a journey to be taken, hence the "road trip" related illustrations throughout; but it is an exciting journey taken with colleagues to achieve something important. I've tried to capture these ideas in the title: "Culture Transformation: Purpose, Passion, Path – Principles for Success."

Widespread transformation will involve the entire team that makes up the organization, and as such the players will stay the same; but their behaviors will undergo some changes. They will be asked to approach work, relationships and accountabilities with different skills and mindsets. As such, their behaviors will be different, and at times possibly quite unfamiliar, but the results will be rewarding, and beneficial.

Getting to that point may well be a significant challenge, and I trust you find the experiences and principles I've shared helpful as you either lead, or participate in, your own culture transformation journey.

# Table of Contents

# Introduction

Culture Transformation can be an exciting time for any organization...it's visible action taken to move from the present to the future. It typically involves many, if not all, of the people in the organization and **has the potential to refocus and reenergize the entire workforce**. It presents a road map of steps being taken to win in a changing world!

But transformation of that magnitude can be challenging. There are many pitfalls lying in wait on the road ahead, and many as yet unidentified opportunities to be seized. Care will be needed to ensure the best of what now exists is secured, and perhaps even amplified, while the areas needing some attention are clearly addressed and truly transformed.

In this book I've attempted to provide my insights into what must be done to ensure success, and the key principles to follow on the journey. Every transformation is as unique as the culture in which it is occurring, so I've avoided being too prescriptive and excessively tactical. Rather, I've attempted to lay out a path forward that will guarantee success if followed, but the individual steps along that path must be tailored to your organization, and the nature of the transformation desired.

People truly are one of any organization's greatest resources, and guiding them to success on the transformation path can be as rewarding for them as for the organization — same talented cast, just a different play!


Phil Geldart

# CULTURE
# TRANSFORMATION
## PURPOSE, PASSION, PATH

### The Principles for Success

# What is Culture, Exactly?

When we look at the culture of an organization we are actually looking at the sum total of the behaviors of all the employees. The corporate culture may have a place in a strategic document somewhere, or be on posters on the walls, but really the **culture is defined by what the people of the organization do**.

It's not sufficient to know what the people in the organization do in general. Culture is more closely aligned to what the people do in particular: that is, in times of stress, at the time of an acquisition, or when the organization is in transition in some fashion. The behavior of the people at these times is what really defines a corporate culture.

It's important to realize that a corporate culture is itself a collection of many cultures.

 *For example, there may be a certain approach to customer service, there may be a unique way of dealing with projects or requests, there may be a specific way of dealing with quality. Each of these areas represents an approach that people adopt, and when taken together define a culture.*

When we think about corporate culture we are really thinking about the way in which each of these aspects of the company is handled, and therefore in their aggregate how the company is defined.

This is critical to understand when we begin to think about culture transformation. A company may not need an entire culture transformation, rather it may only need a transformation in one area; for example, in the area of customer service, or innovation, or in sales.

# The Difference Between Mission, Culture, and Values

Organizations begin with a **Mission**, or Vision. These terms are often used interchangeably, which is fine. Essentially the mission, or vision, states the organization's reason for being. It is a summary which clearly captures the "charter" under which the leadership of the company operates; it is a statement of the "why" the organization exists.

The culture of a company is how the organization brings that mission to life.

**Culture** is the sum total of all the behaviors of the individuals working within that organization. It reflects how they solve problems, how they interact with each other, and how they simply get things done. The operative word here is "how." A culture defines what I'd feel if I joined that organization and had to work there. The things people do (the "how's") create in me a sense of "how I feel things are done here."

Culture is sometimes easy to articulate ("here everyone works long hours"), and sometimes not so easy ("here we just seem to rely a lot on one another"). Either way, those working in that environment get a "feel" for how things are done. They may like it, or not; but either way, they are clear on what it is, and can describe it in some fashion.

**Values**, on the other hand, often provide the basis on which a culture is built. The "value" of "everyone is important" drives an empowering culture. The "value" of "trust experienced leadership above all" drives a more hierarchical culture. The "value" of "integrity" will drive an accountable culture; the value of "respect for an individual's worth" will drive a culture of greater freedom of action.

Clearly an organization's culture is far more complex than just one or two principles, driven by one or two values. Rather it is the sum total of many factors, all in varying degrees.

The key thing, though, is to distinguish between mission, culture, and values. They are different, but mutually dependent; and yet all facets of an organization's identity.

**Mission sets the direction, culture describes how the mission is achieved, and values define what that culture will be.**

When the focus becomes the transformation of a culture, it's important to consider each of these aspects of the organization, and the relative weight of each; then from that perspective determine how best, and what, to alter in order to ensure the newly transformed culture is what's wanted, sustainable, and carrying no unforeseen consequences.

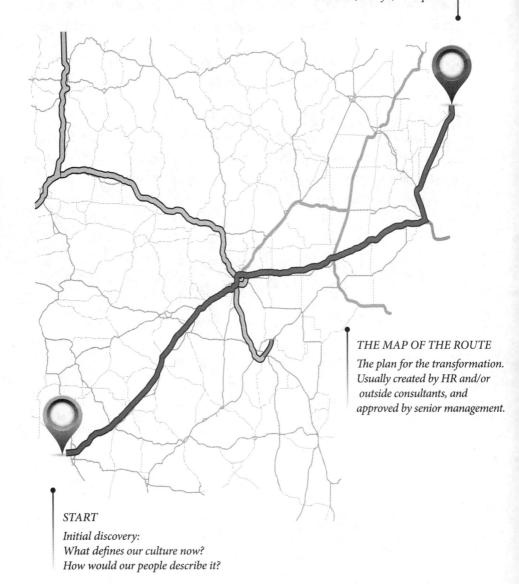

*END*
*After the transformation:*
*How will we be described?*
*What will be the outcome, benefit, or impact?*

*THE MAP OF THE ROUTE*
*The plan for the transformation.*
*Usually created by HR and/or*
*outside consultants, and*
*approved by senior management.*

*START*
*Initial discovery:*
*What defines our culture now?*
*How would our people describe it?*

# Where are We Now?

A transformation of corporate culture must begin with a clear understanding of where the culture is now. There has to be a reason for the organization to want to change the culture in some way, and the more clearly this reason can be articulated the easier it will be to change it.

When taking steps to define the current culture, there are many tools available, as outlined below; but the more important thing is to focus less on the tools, and more on the outcome from using those tools.

Employees who are giving input on the culture, whether they are senior or more junior, need to understand the reason their input is being requested. When seeking input the organization must be willing to encourage an honest and open perspective, allowing others to share exactly how they feel. The reason for this is that if the objective is to change the culture, specific things will need to change. Culture change is not something which occurs in the abstract, but is rather the result of very specific actions.

I mentioned earlier that culture is the sum total of the behaviors of the employees. If that culture is to be changed then behaviors of individuals must change. If the behavior is to change then it must change from something it now is, to something else. In order for this to happen it begins with understanding clearly what the "from" is, before articulating what the "to" should be.

Understanding this comes from the information which is gathered before the culture transformation begins. When this information is specific, and rich with examples and illustrations, then it's much easier to pinpoint why the current culture is the way it is; and then from that to springboard to what the culture should be, as reflected in different behaviors.

When the input tools are being created it is advantageous to include any outside consultants who will be helping with the transformation. Typically, they will have a more objective view, and will help to create tools which are effective at gathering concrete, specific, and objective examples of the current culture.

## THE KINDS OF TOOLS WHICH ARE AVAILABLE ARE AS FOLLOWS:

1. **360° or 180° Surveys.** These are very powerful in that they give the organization a perspective on the way in which leaders are leading the organization, and the impact that leadership style is having on the culture. It is important that these assessments not be used to monitor performance, but rather as a feedback tool to capture current leadership behaviors. The body follows the head, and so clearly any culture is a reflection of the way in which the leaders are leading their teams.

2. **Focus Groups.** These are groups of 5 to 7 people, and should represent employees from all levels. Focus groups typically group people together by levels, and ideally by functions. By doing this it's possible to capture the way in which the various levels of an organization feel about the culture, and specifically how they feel about it in their own area or division. A focus group session typically runs 60 to 90 minutes, and should be structured in such a way as to encourage free-flowing conversation in order to gather information that comes from discussion, rather than from an interview style.

   Several focus groups should be run, as clearly there are many levels within the organization and many divisions, and the viewpoints of each of these needs to be accurately reflected when capturing the existing culture.

*If the organization wishes to focus in on one particular aspect of culture, such as customer service, then the focus group questions should be around that topic. If the organization wishes to change the culture at a larger level, for example around employee engagement, then clearly the questions need to be broader in nature and focus on that larger topic.*

3. **High Potentials.** A group of high potential employees can make up a focus group, or they can be met with individually. The reason for singling out this particular group is that they typically represent the key influencers in an organization, or perhaps even the future leaders. As such their perspective is crucial, and tends to be reasoned, well-balanced, and presented with the best interest of the company in mind. Consequently, selecting the appropriate number, and groups, of high potential's is an important component for gathering accurate input.

4. **Executive One-on-Ones.** Senior management, including the executive group, should also be included. The executives should participate through one-on-one interviews where their opinions can be not only expressed, but examined, discussed in detail, and elaborated upon. They are the leaders of the company and their opinions are crucial. Further, the culture is as a result of the leadership which they are providing, so their perspective on the issue is vital.

5. **World Café.** This is an interactive opportunity for large numbers of people to participate. It can occur either in large meeting rooms where individuals have a chance to move around and give their views either in informal micro discussion sessions, or in writing on large boards set up around the room.

Other techniques for capturing large group input include using digital technology and multi-voting tools. The scope of this form of information gathering can be very expansive and include several hundreds of employees simultaneously.

## COLLECTION AND ANALYSIS OF THE DATA, LEADING TO MEASUREMENT TOOLS

Once the data has been collected the challenge is to do the right thing with it.

The information collected is not intended to be used to find fault, or point fingers. It is not a review of the failings of the current situation. In fact there may be nothing wrong with things as they now are, but rather simply a desire to move to a new and improved state.

**Culture transformation is not always about fixing a problem**. It is much more often about seeing an opportunity or need, and then moving the organization in that direction. Clearly, there are many times when a culture transformation is absolutely vital for survival, or to confront a competitive challenge, but this is not always the case. Equally, often, there's a significant opportunity to be gained by shifting the culture in a new direction. In those cases, it's definitely not about fixing something that's broken, but much more about building something that will take the organization to a more desirable future.

The data collected then needs to be analyzed within that context. The objective is to fully understand the current reality, why the current reality is the way it is, and the key components of that reality which need to change in order for the new future to be realized. The input which has been gathered reflects how the people who live the culture feel, are behaving, and believe they have to perform. Once this has been understood it can then be codified and steps taken to change what is necessary, while still keeping what is good and desirable.

Analysis of the data can fall into a number of categories. **The first is the most obvious one: measurement**. There will undoubtedly be several metrics which surface that can be used to reflect either the current culture or the outcome of that culture. Identifying these metrics, and then determining their current status, will provide an initial baseline, and an opportunity to identify targets for these metrics in the future as the transformation unfolds.

The importance of measuring the outcome, and not simply the related activities, is critical. Very often metrics measure things which people do, but it is the actual output of a culture that's most critical. Consequently, the metrics must be focused on measuring the output, or the impact, or the results of the activities of individuals.

When creating metrics for the outputs of the new culture very often existing metrics can often contribute, but will not be fully complete. In that case the data collected may point the way to creating some new metrics which will be very helpful in measuring progress towards the final goal, and indicating when success has been achieved.

The question is often asked: "Which are the most important metrics to use when creating a culture change?" My response is "Ask the CFO." The CFO is responsible to the CEO and the shareholders for reporting on the health, progress, and profitability of the enterprise. As such the CFO has key metrics which are used in that reporting. If the culture is to change or be transformed in some way then clearly the metrics on which the CFO reports should improve. Given that the transformed culture is really to be the sum total of the behaviors of the individuals within the organization, the results of those new behaviors should contribute to the results on which the CFO reports. Consequently, any change which is made to the culture should be reflected in the metrics which are used to monitor the health, progress, and success of the organization.

This view – using the CFO's existing metrics – often raises eyebrows as people believe that a culture transformation is typically something more behavior-based, and in the soft skills area, than something which is related to the hard-nosed metrics of the CFO. However, the culture transformation must impact the company's success and so those metrics must be part of what's used to track the progress of the transformation.

**A second focus for measurement is rooted in the fact that a successful transformation is dependent on the leaders of that organization**. Without the full involvement and commitment of their line managers then the individuals that make up the organization will not adopt the necessary behaviors that the new culture requires. Consequently, it is absolutely vital that each manager, at every level within the organization, be committed, aligned, and focused on making the new culture a reality.

As such, metrics must be in place to track the level of engagement of those leaders. These metrics are typically gathered through some form of assessment provided by each leader's team members. The only way to truly determine the effectiveness of a leader is to look at the performance of those they lead, and consider their input. Hence, an assessment of the leadership should be included in the metrics related to the culture transformation. The input which has been collected earlier will help to identify which behaviors the leaders should demonstrate, and that therefore should be included on the assessment.

**The third area of metrics are those related to the behaviors of individuals other than those related to leadership**. While these are often related to activities rather than results, they are still important and they will still help to determine whether or not progress is being made towards the new culture.

 *For example, if the culture is attempting to move towards being more innovative, one of the behaviors required is involvement in regular innovation meetings to generate ideas, and then to pursue those ideas through to completion. A behavior that could then be measured is the number of meetings held, attendance at those meetings, number of ideas generated, and then presented; another could be around the percentage of ideas which are pursued through to implementation.*

This is simply an example of the way in which a new behavior can be measured, and then linked to the overall desired outcome of the culture transformation.

As a result of the input which has been received before the transformation begins there will be much greater clarity around why the culture is currently the way it is. An analysis of this will then help to determine what different kinds of activities are necessary to achieve a different kind a result, or move the culture in the direction desired, and so help to create the most accurate metrics.

From this, the necessary training plans are built to equip each individual with the skills necessary to demonstrate the new behaviors, create the new culture, and so change the measured results.

There is more detail around measurement later in the book in the "Measurement" chapter.

**MOUNTAIN PASSES**
*Some aspects of the transformation will be much harder (uphill going!) than others (downhill going!). Stay the course, it's simply part of the journey.*

# Do We Really Need a Transformation in the First Place?

The organization currently produces a product or service for customers or consumers. This product or service is provided within a competitive marketplace, an economic environment, a political climate, and a marketplace reality.

The products and services are the result of the corporate culture which pervades the entire organization, and the many smaller cultures which are in evidence within functions and departments, and within corporate priorities.

 *For example, the marketing department may have a slightly different culture from the sales department; or the culture around customer service may be different from the culture around internal processes, in that a high-priority may be placed on servicing external customers but a low priority placed on serving one another internally.*

When looking at opportunities, both in the near-term and the long-term, management may believe that a culture transformation would be of benefit. In fact, it may not be just the opinion of management, but the Board may in fact require a culture transformation; or outside bodies may demand some form of culture transformation; or results from surveys such as customer feedback data may indicate the need for a culture transformation. Any one of several sources may trigger the need for action. **The desired transformation may not need to encompass the entire organization, but rather need only to be focused on a single area** (e.g., manufacturing or supply chain). Whatever the focal point, or the identified need, some form of culture shift has been indicated as being required.

It is difficult to stress enough that the culture is the sum total of the behaviors of the individuals; and that the results being obtained are the consequences of those behaviors. If the results are unacceptable, behaviors must change, and in that case the culture must change.

This then leads to the question: **"What, exactly, is a culture transformation really, and how will I know when it has been achieved?"**

The exact nature of a culture transformation is simply that the people within the organization are behaving differently in some fashion, on a consistent basis, and that different behavior is being supported by each manager. The results of adopting those new behaviors will result in improved metrics, or outcomes consistent with what has been determined as essential for the long-term success, and maybe even survival, of the organization. The culture transformation will be achieved when the desired results, or metrics have been achieved.

A culture transformation is therefore a process whereby, over time, people behave differently and the organization benefits in some fashion as a result. If these benefits are required, then a transformation is necessary.

This is not easy to achieve.

People have been equipped, trained, reinforced, motivated, recognized, and conditioned over time to behave in a certain fashion. The larger the organization the more deep-rooted these behaviors are. To change these behaviors is challenging because all the things that had previously created the current behaviors have left their mark and are still working against that change. When change is initiated people lose a sense of clarity as to which behaviors are going to be rewarded, which recognized, and which become a priority. When a culture transformation is initiated people tend to lose their cultural compass in terms of knowing the right way to behave in all circumstances.

When change of this magnitude occurs people look to their leaders for help and direction, but these leaders are themselves also involved in the change and so may not be able to provide adequate help. Often organizations are a blend of many cultures. New employees have brought the cultural thinking from their previous employment, or an acquisition has brought that culture into the mix. It's quite conceivable that all of these cultures are still settling and trying to find roots within the larger corporate organization. This compounds the problem. Further, it is quite conceivable that the existing culture is itself not fully understood by all, at all times and in all circumstances, for example in a widespread or global organization.

Consequently, a disciplined approach to culture transformation needs to be implemented. This disciplined approach has many facets, but has a single objective: the aligning of every employee and every leader towards a given direction in terms of what to do, and how to do it, in order to achieve an expected outcome.

# Creating a Line of Sight

The reason for the culture transformation, or the benefit of its successful implementation, can be highly motivating. When **people understand the benefits** that will occur as a result of a successful transformation, or even during the journey, **then they are much more willing and able to support all the efforts that are required to achieve it**. This understanding of the benefits is the far end of a line. The current situation is the near end of the same line. By joining these two points we create a line of sight from where we are to where we're going.

When this line of sight is very apparent to individuals, and they are each easily able to identify the benefit of the transformation, then this provides a framework, or a backdrop, against which every aspect of the transformation can be communicated. For someone to remain engaged, and willing to undergo the changes which a transformation requires, then this line of sight must be absolutely clear. Typically, this is done well in the early stages but is lost over time. Those driving the transformation make the assumption that once the line of sight has been laid down for people then it provides a constant reference point. This is not true.

In the early days when the line is clearly articulated, it does provide a strong point of reference for people. However, over time, things happen. The line of sight is a bit like trail markers on a path, which are initially very clear, easy to see, and mark the newly cut path.

*MILE MARKERS*
*Previously identified metrics used as key indicators of progress and crucial to achieve.*

However, without constant grooming the path can become overgrown, lost, or washed out. Without attention the trail markers can become faded, or lost.

That which was so clear in the beginning has somehow in later days become fuzzy, or obscured, or no longer visible. Similarly, the line of sight between where we are and where we are going can become less obvious. It is no longer something to which individuals can consistently refer.

If the opposite remains true, and the line of sight is frequently referenced and refreshed then people are willing to stay on the path, and push towards the end, knowing clearly that the effort is worthwhile, and their energy well spent.

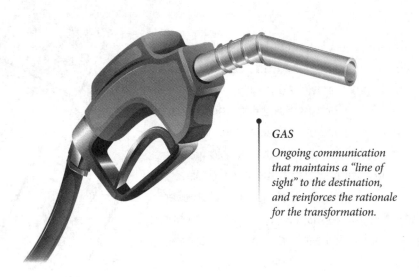

**GAS**

*Ongoing communication that maintains a "line of sight" to the destination, and reinforces the rationale for the transformation.*

# The Role of Leadership

In any culture transformation **leadership is absolutely vital. It is the difference between success and failure.** Within any organization people follow their leaders.

The question is often asked: "Are we talking about the most senior leadership of the company that is, the executive team, or middle-management, or the front-line supervisors?" The answer is: "All levels."

If the organizational focus is on a company-wide culture transformation, then the CEO and the executive team have to be fully involved. On the other hand, if the organizational focus is simply on a culture change within a division, then only the divisional head needs to be seen as its leader. Similarly, if the culture transformation is occurring at a local level, such as a distribution center, then the head of the distribution center needs to be fully involved. The principle is that the most senior individual in the area undergoing a transformation needs to spearhead the initiative.

This does not mean that the most senior person needs to be personally involved in every aspect of the transformation, or visible at every situation where the transformation is being addressed. Very often the transformation can be implemented by a team, but those affected must recognize that the most senior person is fully aware of the transformation being implemented, is fully supportive of it, and personally as fully engaged in the transformation as all other individuals are expected to be.

It is important to recognize that the mechanics, or tactics, of any transformation will require a considerable amount of administrative effort and focus. Communication will have to be provided, training will have to occur, classes will have to be scheduled, memos written and videos created. Clearly, each of these can be done by a team of individuals who are focused on the transformation, but it is absolutely vital to realize that the transformation team are not the ones responsible for the outcome. They are responsible for the tactics, but not the outcome. **The leaders are responsible for the outcome**.

The most senior person should be relying on the implementation team for direction, for insight, and often for clarity as to where best to spend his or her time. The senior person is looking for the same level of support and help on the transformation that they might also be looking for from a head of Legal on legal matters, or from a head of Finance on financial issues.

As with any responsibility, **the person responsible must be an example of the behaviors that are required**. In a transformation typically these are new and different, and may not come any more easily to those in senior positions.

The leader must also be there to help support and coach where necessary. The leader must have as a nonnegotiable imperative that the new behaviors are something which every individual must adopt, and embrace. Without stepping up to this degree, and being seen to step up and lead the transformation, it will not be effective, or be only partially effective. It is critical for these leaders to understand the challenge and importance of first changing their own behavior if the transformation is actually going to occur. They need to model what they want to see in others.

This is also a challenge because transformation is not something which happens quickly, or easily. Rather it will take time, focus, and energy. People need to learn new ways of behaving, practice with them, overcome the natural problems they will encounter in attempting to adopt new behaviors, and work with them until they become habitual.

Without the leader's focus, and sustained attention on making sure that these behaviors actually remain top of mind, and helping people master them, it will be easy for individuals to slip back into their earlier ways of behaving, to stay rooted in the past, in ways which have previously been rewarded, and are typically more comfortable.

Within a culture transformation the senior people are the ones that should be providing the motivation for success. They should be reinforcing the rationale for the transformation. They should be front and center in encouraging people to persevere when it's difficult to adopt the new behaviors. In addition, they must demonstrate clearly that they are committed to the long-term sustained effort that any transformation will take.

This responsibility falls to every leader, not just the senior ones. It definitely begins with senior leadership, because they set the tone and the pace, but it must then cascade down to every level of leadership. This, in itself, is a challenge.

Below the senior-level the understanding of the need for the transformation is often not as clear. The senior team often best understands it and is willing to support it, invest in it, and do what is necessary to make it happen; but they have not been adequately effective at communicating the reason for the transformation.

*GPS*

*Senior management's visible support and leadership of the transformation.*

Consequently, as the responsibility for living these new behaviors cascades throughout the organization other leaders may not accept it is as readily and completely as the senior leaders do.

It is **critical that every level of leadership is able to demonstrate that they fully embrace and support the transformation.** A challenge to this happening is that typically, as the leadership responsibilities move down through the company, leaders are increasingly less skilled, both in terms of communication and staff development. They're not as effective at communicating the rationale for any change of this magnitude, nor are they as able to provide the necessary support and coaching to help their own people adopt these new behaviors.

It is often the case that the transformation will fail not because the senior people are not fully committed to it, but rather that they have underestimated what is required to engage the leaders below their level all the way down to the frontline supervisor in the leadership of this initiative. It is therefore vital to focus a significant portion of the training on the leadership below the senior-level; to give them the skills, and often the conviction, necessary for them to provide the support the organization will need.

To underestimate the level of intensity of training required to make this happen would be a mistake. It is obviously important to train the employees of the organization on the new behaviors required by the transformation, but it is far more important to train the leaders of those employees around their role, and to give them both the skill and the confidence necessary so they can be seen to lead the transformation, and in fact to lead it.

Within an organization the culture transformation is the responsibility of leadership.

*Any aspect of any business is ultimately the responsibility of leadership. The effective running of the warehouse is the responsibility of the warehouse supervisor; the outcome of the sales team is the responsibility of the sales manager; and a successful closing of the books at year-end is the responsibility of the controller or head of finance. All leaders carry the responsibility for their functions to ensure that the expectations of the organization are met as required. A culture transformation is no different. It's the responsibility of leaders to ensure that this transformation, and the expected outcomes, are delivered as expected, and as required.*

Simply because it is something that is perhaps new, or requiring skills that are not in their natural complement of skill sets, does not mean that they are not responsible for the successful implementation of the transformation. They are.

It then becomes the responsibility of the team charged with implementing this transformation to ensure that they provide the necessary training and support that each of these leaders will require. They must ensure that the transformation begins at the leadership level, and that leaders are equipped to be successful in this area. The current culture is as a result of the current leadership. If the culture is to change, the leaders must change, and the implementation team must show the leaders how this is to happen. They must provide senior management with the regular feedback they need to support it happening, and be able to demonstrate the patience required for it to happen. Learning these new behaviors will take time, and that must be clearly understood, both by those who wish to see it happen, and by those who are learning to make it happen.

# The Challenge of Transformation

**Culture transformation is not for the faint of heart**. There are many hurdles to successful transformation, not the least of which is the determination to stay the course. We are all familiar with the phrase, "flavor of the month," and this very often describes initiatives begun within organizations but which do not come to fruition for one reason or another.

*HURDLES*

*Some hurdles may appear which could block progress. Identify the hurdle and quickly find a response to sustain the focus on the transformation.*

Once management undertakes to do something, it always seems like the right thing to do at the time, and it is always begun with enthusiasm. However, once underway there often seems to be a wide array of things lurking in wait to waylay that initiative, or move it lower on the priority list. An acquisition, a challenge in the marketplace, a new competitor, or just the day-to-day urgencies of business, are all things which can intervene to take any initiative and move it from center stage into the wings.

Like anything else, culture transformation can easily be sidetracked. However, unlike other initiatives, the consequences of doing so are much more severe. Once underway a culture transformation has made clear to the organization that there is dissatisfaction with the current state and that steps are being taken to change it.

If done well, this early communication and messaging will be clear, have been cascaded throughout the entire organization, and have engaged people's hearts and enthusiasm around the change. They have essentially bought in to the idea of the transformation, and in general, are willing to embrace it.

Given this, to then allow this transformation to take a lower place on the agenda, or receive a lower priority, is the equivalent of saying to the organization; "Either we were wrong in the first place, or it is not as important as we originally said." Chances are that neither of these things are true, but rather that somehow the transformation initiative has simply slipped either off the radar screen, or more likely just not received the same level of attention in its later stages as it did when it was initially begun.

This then identifies the **first major hurdle to culture transformation: the need to stay the course**. Unlike other initiatives typically a culture transformation will take 2 to 4 years, and throughout that time will require the sustained focus and attention that it initially received. The focus on culture transformation must continue despite all the possible hindrances or distractions which can occur. Once begun, people need to know that senior management remains fully committed to the sustained effort required to see the transformation fully implemented. This is not easy, and we as humans tend to want to move on to new things once old things are underway and seem to be moving well. This is a good approach in most cases, but with culture transformation, not so. Every day the full journey of culture transformation must see the same degree of focus and effort if the ultimate result is to be achieved.

The **second major consideration** is the other side of the same coin, and that is a **recognition that true transformation will not occur quickly, nor easily**. True, some individuals will embrace it immediately and make change almost instantly. However, for the majority of the organization it will take time. People will need to understand what is meant by the change, and what new behaviors are required; they'll need to learn these new behaviors, and then learn to apply them.

Then there is a small percentage of each organization that will be extremely slow to adopt a new way of behaving, if at all. They present their own challenges.

To begin a culture transformation is to recognize right from the outset that the journey will be one of a number of years, and that patience must be demonstrated as people understand what is required and how to behave. Given our desire to want to tackle new things, to give into other competing priorities, and the frustrations which can occur when others seem to take longer than we would like to acquire these new behaviors, it is easy to see why a culture transformation can falter.

Over time the actual transformation initiative is frequently still "officially important," but it has been delegated. It has been passed on to someone two or three layers below those who were initially involved with spearheading its successful implementation. Management has decided that it is now well underway, and no longer needs their personal attention. They believe it will happen now if simply "managed."

This must not be allowed to happen. Otherwise it will slowly, and unintentionally, have become another "flavor of the month." Rather, it must remain a high priority, and senior management must stay involved. It must be clear to the organization that the determination to see the culture move from what it is to what it needs to be has not wavered in the face of other priorities, or other situations. Once this conviction is in place it is much more likely to see continued results, and in due course an acceleration of those results.

# New Behaviors

I frequently reference the fact that a **culture transformation will require the learning of new behaviors**. This is because all activities which occur within an organization by people are really the sum total of the ways in which they behave in a variety of circumstances, which in turn defines an organization's culture.

 *If the culture is one that is described as fast-paced, aggressive, and "every person for themselves," then clearly the behaviors which one would see in that culture reflect people making decisions quickly, taking action quickly, moving to places and outcomes which tend to be more focused on the benefit to be realized for themselves than for others. This would describe an organization where internal competition is encouraged, where time spent in discussion and collaboration would be at a minimum, and where individual prowess is recognized above all. The common view of a trader in the financial markets would tend to fit this description.*

*On the other hand if the culture is one that is collaborative, thoughtful, others-centered, and caring, then the kinds of behaviors one would tend to see here are those that would encourage meeting together, considering alternatives, acting only after the impact on others is considered, and after considerable thought has been given to the impact on the needs or quality of life of others. Here, the general view of humanitarian focused organizations, or those concerned about the well-being of those deeply in need, come to mind.*

Whatever the situation, the culture of an organization is no more than the behaviors of its members. If the culture requires a transformation of some sort, then the behaviors must change.

*A compassionate and caring culture may feel that it needs to become somewhat more efficient, and aware of the need to move more quickly. In that case the transformation requires that all the qualities which are valued are kept, but that individual behaviors change so that they also include ways to be more efficient, and actions which demonstrate a greater attention being paid to time management. This is a good example of a culture transformation that needs to occur, and would benefit many, but which does not require the organization to change its entire culture completely. Rather, a portion of that culture needs some attention, and steps need to be taken to address it. Rarely does an organization need to transform its entire culture. Much more frequently, it is merely some aspect of the larger culture which requires attention.*

*Other examples: a service industry may feel that its attention to customer service has waned so a transformation is required that brings much greater attention to the customers, and so become more customer centric. A fast food operation may feel as though their focus on hygiene has slipped, so the transformation's focus is to drive each individual to be more attentive to presenting cleanliness as a key differentiator. A manufacturing operation may feel that a transformation around safety is vital as some situations have occurred which have made management feel as though safety is no longer high enough on the priority list.*

Whatever the situation, the behaviors of the individuals involved must change. This then leads to the question: **"How to change behavior?"**

There are a **number of components** that are necessary, and over the course of this book, they are all addressed. One which has already been discussed is the **involvement of senior management to lead and support the new behaviors**. Another is **maintaining a clear line of sight** as to why the new behaviors need to change. However, there is a **third and vital element** which must be involved, and that is **training**.

The training of individuals is an incredibly powerful way to change behavior. Training that is done well, that engages individual's hearts as well as their minds, which includes practice and a focus on results as well as the simple sharing of knowledge, can have an outstanding effect on changing human behavior. This training must be done with care, since training can actually change the entire direction of an organization, and radically influence the outcomes which are being obtained and the value which is being given to the shareholders.

Typically, if individuals are shown how to behave differently from their norm, which is then seen to be better, and they adopt those new ways, performance improves.

 *This is true in sports such as golf, tennis, or swimming when new skills are learned and practiced until they are habitual. It is true in areas such as drama, pottery, or painting; and it is true in technical areas such as plumbing, welding, or machine repair. Virtually every endeavor with which we are involved can be impacted positively by training; with training we can learn to be better athletes, better craftsmen, or more technically skilled.*

There are some forms of training that are dramatically more effective than others. There are organizations offering leadership training which has limited effect, and there are organizations offering leadership training which is highly effective. There are those who are very poor at training their apprentices, and those who are brilliant at it. There is no question that the quality of training varies widely, but this does not take away from the fact that training can be the best possible way to change human behavior, and that great training can make a great difference.

If this principle is applied to culture transformation, then obviously training is a critical component. Individuals within the organization undergoing a transformation must be trained in terms of what new behaviors are expected, and how to demonstrate them.

**REARVIEW MIRROR**
*Competitive activity in the marketplace.*

**OTHER OCCUPANTS**
*Immediate supervisor (line manager), mentors, transformation support staff, colleagues.*

**IN-CAR ENTERTAINMENT**
*An intentional focus on ensuring the transformation journey remains engaging and positive.*

**THE DRIVER**
*Each individual within the organization.*

**THE CAR**
*The way work is being done every day.*

Once the training has been provided, then the line manager steps in. The line manager's job is to work with their own teams in terms of the application of the training on the job. Essentially this requires that the line manager focus on three areas: **what to stop**; **what to start**; and **what to continue**. This three-part test is extremely valuable to line managers as they provide help along the path towards the transformation of the culture.

This help should be in the form of a discussion about day-to-day priorities, how they are affected by this focus on the culture transformation, and what behaviors are currently being demonstrated which are no longer consistent with the new culture desired, and can therefore be stopped.

Discussion then moves to what behaviors are currently not being demonstrated which have been learned in the recent training, and should now become part of the day-to-day activities. These need to start.

Then thirdly, what portion of current behaviors are fine, and remain crucial to the way in which we operate, and, as such, are not to be affected by the transformation.

 *An example of this would be an organization wishing to transform its sales force from farmers to hunters. In this example, the culture of the organization is strong, and most aspects of the organization are what they should be in the eyes of senior management. However, for some reason, perhaps competitive pressure, or the launch of a new product, senior management feels that the sales force culture of essentially being order takers is no longer adequate. They must move to being a more aggressive sales force seeking new business and finding new clients...essentially moving from farmers to hunters.*

*For members of the sales force this is a significant culture transformation. Individuals who used to come to work clear in terms of how they did their job, would have described the culture as one where the role was about relationships and taking orders on a regular basis. Now the culture is changing, sales reps must be more aggressive, they need to reach out and find new business, and spend less time over coffee maintaining relationships, and more time finding new customers to sell to. For each rep this is a dramatic culture transformation.*

*In this example, each sales manager needs to sit with their reps and reinforce that the way in which business was done before now needs to shift. The things which need to stop are things which relate to the attitude of being merely an order taker, and working the same route. The things which need to be initiated relate to building a base of new people to talk to, spending more time tracking down potential new customers, and then presenting the company's products to them. The things which need to continue are focus on quality, service, attention to detail, and reputation.*

While this is only a summary of a conversation which would take much longer, and include far more, it does provide an illustration of **"stop, start, continue."** There will be things within the current organization which are great and need to continue, but for the transformation to occur other things must be discontinued, and now be replaced with new behaviors that will produce different results.

# The Importance of Inclusiveness

When launching any form of culture transformation it is **important to include everybody**. I'm often asked whether or not a culture transformation can be started with a small group and then expanded, or whether it can be "tested" in some fashion. Clearly these are options, and have value. However, in my opinion, for a true transformation to occur it must be well thought out in advance, and then launched on a widespread basis.

There is a very practical reason for including everybody immediately: individuals within an organization are interconnected. Imagine that someone with whom you work is attempting to adopt new behaviors as a result of the culture transformation, and yet you have no appreciation or understanding of those new behaviors. You immediately wonder why they're doing what they're doing, and why they are not doing what they used to do; you may wonder why you are not getting what you used to get, or why you're now getting things you never used to receive. Priorities of those around you have shifted, or their behavior towards you has changed in some fashion. These are all mystifying, and while you may clearly understand it has something to do with "culture transformation," you certainly don't understand it, and so cannot support or embrace it. Your life has suddenly become far more difficult.

When the transformation is not all-encompassing, then colleagues working side-by-side are working with different priorities, different behavioral expectations, and different outcomes. They are not all united towards a common purpose and a common outcome, and this results in inefficiency, frustration, lack of productivity and "water cooler" talk. If a transformation is required, then everyone affected by the transformation should be involved from the outset, and all at the same time.

In practice not everybody can take the relevant training at exactly the same time, and people understand that. But everyone should be registered for the training at the same time, and know that they will all be participating over the coming weeks so that they know they will be involved, and part of the initiative. Including everybody is essential if the organization is looking to see the behaviors of everybody change. Leaving people out, or delaying their participation, is counterproductive.

 *If the transformation is focused, for example at a manufacturing site, then not everybody in the company needs to be nearly as involved as those at the site. Most areas that support it will need some appreciation for what the transformation is achieving, and therefore their role in supporting it, but beyond that their need to be involved is much more limited. However, if the transformation is to be widespread across the entire organization, then everyone needs to be involved, and preferably at the same time.*

In other words, if the culture transformation is directed towards a specific group, not everybody would need to have the same training as that group. However, those directly connected to this group will need some training, and some clarity in terms of how they are to support the new behaviors. This shorter program can explain the transformation occurring within a targeted group: what to expect, what others will do differently, and how they can best support them.

This is somewhat like dropping a rock in a pond. In the immediate center, where the rock is dropped, is where the transformation has to occur; but as the waves ripple out there is less and less impact until finally some distance from that center there is limited impact. In the same way, for a transformation that is focused on only one area of the business not every area requires the same level of focus. Those increasingly remote from the area of focus need some attention, but proportionately less and less.

# The Need for Conviction

I referred earlier to the importance of training as a key component for culture transformation, and that the training has to be optimally effective. Whether conviction is included as part of the training or occurs elsewhere, it must nonetheless be a significant component of the plan for culture transformation.

**By conviction, I mean that the hearts and passions of the people need to be engaged**. Emotions are a vital part of who we are as human beings, and a powerful motivator. To attempt any form of transformation, especially a cultural one, without paying significant attention to the need to include a focus on building personal conviction would be ineffective.

As individuals go about their day-to-day work they carry with them certain beliefs, and certain convictions related to the organization. They are proud to be associated with the company; or they believe passionately in the products; or they stay with that company because of what it does for others; or they are convinced that this is the most effective way to provide for their families, their well-being, and their own personal priorities. Whatever they are, people carry convictions with them every day while at work.

Sometimes these convictions are extremely helpful and vital to an organization. The conviction that their organization is among the best in the industry in which they compete builds pride; sometimes the conviction is that their product or service is unique, and doing a great service to the world; sometimes simply the conviction that this is the best possible place to earn a living is important. As human beings we make many decisions based virtually entirely on conviction or emotion; from how we spend our leisure time, to whom we decide to spend our life with, to where we choose to work. Whatever they are, the convictions which we have as individuals drive us to action, or commitment, or the decisions as to whether to stay at a company or leave it; or to determine how we interact with our colleagues, or customers, or others within the company.

Our activities and behaviors are influenced by the things which we believe, not simply by the things which we know. **If we do not fully value the beliefs which people have, and the degree to which those convictions and beliefs will drive them towards action or inaction, we are missing a crucial component of behavior change.**

I talked earlier about a "line of sight" between where the company now is, and where it wishes to be.

*If, for example, an organization wishes to create a line of sight between the current reality of "less profitable" to a new reality of "more profitable," then conviction around the value of achieving that new reality - being more profitable - is very important. "Why are we doing this?" "What is the benefit?" "Will it affect me?" "Will it affect our customers?" "Who else will it affect?" "What happens if we don't do it?" "Why didn't we do it before?" All these questions surface, but they are all rooted more in emotion than in intellect. If it is simply a matter of providing the answers to the questions then they could be presented in 10 or 15 minutes on a PowerPoint. However, if the expectation is that behavior will change, and change permanently, then people truly need to viscerally grasp the answers to these questions, and understand why their behavior needs to change as a result.*

Consequently, any culture transformation needs to include a significant component around changing people's convictions or beliefs. This is not something which is Machiavellian, or has to be done with some form of subterfuge. Rather, there are clear approaches that can help change personal convictions in a way that is transparent, respectful, and value-based.

*For example, if the objective is to move towards a culture of greater profitability, then asking individuals within the organization to participate in an experience or work through a simulation that mirrors the current reality can help greatly.*

*If it also mirrors the future reality where much greater profit is achieved it can help people understand for themselves what components need to change to produce more profit; and the long term impact of doing so. They thereby develop a personal appreciation of the benefit of achieving it, and the undesirable consequences of merely maintaining the status quo.*

People may understand intellectually why more profit is needed, but they probably do not understand how it affects them personally, and may have no conviction that they can meaningfully change it. However, when participating in a simulation or experiential activity that shows they can each play a significant role, and fully understand how their functional area can contribute, then they are far more motivated to engage on that journey.

A powerful motivational speaker can certainly build passion and conviction, but it is temporary and fleeting. If the motivational speaker is to maintain that level of emotional engagement for an extended period of time, then the listener has to be in the presence of that speaker almost continuously to be influenced by the motivational speaker's passion. This may ultimately produce conviction, but even then it is questionable whether the listener has actually formed sustainable personable convictions.

However, if an individual goes through a personal experience that mirrors the intended transformation, and has a chance to discuss at length various viewpoints, then that level of personal involvement and engagement builds conviction. **People learn by doing, by being engaged and involved**. Consequently, **any culture transformation must allow time for conviction to build, and be reinforced continually**. Experiential learning and simulations can go a long way to providing the basis for discussion, self-reflection, and coming to a personal point of choice. This is what builds conviction and provides a foundation for the future activities that follow, as the transformation then moves to building skills based on that conviction.

**RAINSTORMS**
*A period when there are many competing priorities co-existing with the transformation.*

**CLEAR DAY**
*No corporate issues to cloud the focus. Take advantage of it.*

**FOG EVERYWHERE**
*The vision for the transformation seems lost, or unfocussed. Engage senior management ("the GPS") to quickly move back into a place of clarity and purpose.*

*Another example: an organization may need to become more productive. Current behavior is no longer adequate in today's competitive market. However, most people feel as though they are doing all that they can, and are as productive as possible. To ask them to change will receive nods of understanding, and people may well agree that it is a great objective, (maybe for someone else!) but will not have any conviction that they actually can personally change significantly or perhaps that they even need to change. This is partly because they don't know how to change, and partly because they don't fully understand the principles upon which increased productivity are based.*

By putting them through an experience which allows them to see their own behavior and measure the productivity of that, and then see that other behaviors are possible and the significantly improved productivity that results from those behaviors, conviction is built. People come away from that kind of experience realizing that it is possible to change and to learn how to change. They are now more open to change when they see that it can be done, and they have acquired a personal conviction that new behaviors are possible and attainable.

In this way, some form of activity that engages people, and allows them to do things and draw conclusions for themselves, is a powerful way in which to build conviction, and reach beyond the intellect into the emotions.

Another way to support this objective is for **senior management to be visible, and constantly repeating the message of the transformation and its rationale**. When senior management are visible, and consistent in their messaging, then those individuals within the company that are the most highly respected (senior management) are sending a message with which others will identify, and of which they want to be a part. When the message is transparent, honest, and consistently repeated, then conviction is built regarding its importance, and it begins to affect how others feel, think and act.

Again, I often feel as though we underestimate the importance and impact of senior management on shaping behavior and beliefs. An organization takes on the complexion of its management. If that management wishes people to behave in a different fashion, and develop convictions around the importance of new behaviors, then those leading need to show that they both know, and truly believe in, what they are asking of others.

One of the challenges organizations face is that senior management will often have this conviction, but then need to rely on layers of leadership below to carry the message. It is the kiss of death when leaders two or three layers below say things like: "They say we have to do this," or "This is the message I was told to communicate," or worst of all, "I do not agree, but I have to tell you this." It is absolutely vital that every layer of management demonstrates that they are personally convinced as to the need for the culture transformation, and the steps being taken to achieve it. When they communicate this message then it will succeed. As fire kindles fire, so passion kindles conviction.

The third way to support building conviction within an organization is to **ensure that the human resource practices of the organization are aligned with the new behaviors**. When individuals are promoted because they demonstrate the new behaviors, when individuals are recruited into an organization because they have qualities consistent with the new behaviors, when the performance management systems reflect feedback against the new behaviors, and when the high potential program reflects the importance of demonstrating the new behaviors, then the organization quickly realizes that the company is serious about these new behaviors. People realize that to be successful going forward they must clearly develop their own convictions around the culture transformation, it's benefit, and the need for all to demonstrate it.

Too often a culture transformation occurs in isolation from all the other practices related to the people of the company. A culture transformation is simply a matter of changing the behaviors of people, and as such every aspect of people management should be touched by it. Conviction will follow when each individual feels as though the practices, policies and procedures of the company are all aligned against these new behaviors. They will then understand its importance, and begin to develop the beliefs that are necessary to fully commit to learning and applying the new behaviors necessary for the transformation to occur.

When these three tools are brought to bear: experiential learning, senior management visibility, and aligned HR practices, conviction will grow.

*CAR MAINTENANCE*
*Leader led reinforcement activities done periodically*
*by each leader with their own teams.*

# Timing

A culture transformation, even one done on a smaller scale for only a single department, will take several months, and for a company-wide one as long as four years.

There are several reasons for this. **Firstly, it always takes time for people to understand what's expected of them, then learn the new behaviors, and then put them into practice**. It's this putting into practice which can often extend the life of a transformation. For those involved in a culture transformation not only must they internalize and fully understand how to behave according to the new intentions, but they also need to understand how to behave in several different situations and circumstances.

**SLOWER CARS**
*Be patient. Not everyone will learn and adapt at the same pace.*

An individual may go to training to learn, but it is only in the practice and the application of that learning that they fully grasp the implications and intent behind the learning. Further, many people need to be convinced that the organization is serious about the new behaviors before they will even begin to consider adopting them. Often times people will "sit in the bleachers," or "on the fence," and wait until they are sure that this new way of behaving will in fact become the norm. They, in effect, assume that any initiative will be temporary, and that it too will pass. As a result, it can be a number of months before they fully commit to attempting to adopt new behaviors for themselves, let alone master them.

It's for this reason that those leading the transformation must be patient, and recognize that it will take time.

**The transformation also takes time because not everyone learns at the same pace**. Some learn more quickly than others, some adapt more quickly than others, and with all the best intentions in the world some people are just simply slower to pick up what is expected and begin to apply it.

In these circumstances it is important not to judge all those individuals who are slower on the uptake as unwilling, or fence-sitting as resisting the transformation. Often it is simply that they have either not had an opportunity to actually apply the new behaviors, or enough of an opportunity to use them consistently until they have become habitual. Whatever the case, the learning will take time, and management must allow individuals this time.

**The third reason for the time required is that with any transformation it is not simply one behavior which needs to change**. Usually there are several things which are being addressed, and changing simultaneously. Each of these must be learned, absorbed, internalized, and then applied. Hence, one area of the transformation must be presented at a time, and explained, then time given for that topic to be understood and applied. Then another presented, and so on, until the full range of transformation issues have been covered.

It is understanding that a transformation is really going to require a considerable number of things to change that causes those responsible to set aside a number of years for the transformation to occur. Individuals need to learn for themselves how to behave in the new world, how to interact with others, how to interact with those they lead or are led by, and how to interact with customers, either internal or external. They need to learn how to use new forms, policies, procedures, or metrics, and how and where to take initiative. This is a lot to absorb in the course of the normal activity of the job. For a real transformation to occur each of these topics needs to be covered, and then time given before the next topic is presented. Then once each topic has been covered, time needs to be allowed for them to gel into an integrated whole, so that individuals can see how they all work together and are interconnected.

With this understanding those acting as architects for the transformation can then lay out a plan, and set aside the time required for it to happen.

Once the behaviors are in place, and the organization is feeling the benefit, then a focus has to be on **maintaining these new behaviors,** and **staying the course until they become habitual within the company.**

 *As an example, if I were to pour a glass of water on the carpet it would darken it, and the carpet would appear stained. However, when I return 24 hours later the water will have evaporated and the stain would have vanished. On the other hand, if I pour a bottle of India ink on the carpet, it would also appear to be stained; but in this case when I return in 24 hours, or 24 months, the stain will still be there. A culture transformation needs to have the same long-term impact as the India ink, and creating that level of permanence takes time.*

**CITY DRIVING**

*Times when the requirements of the business (e.g., year end) simply slow everything down, including the transformation activities.*

**COUNTRY DRIVING**

*Times when nothing stands in the way of accelerating the culture transformation activities.*

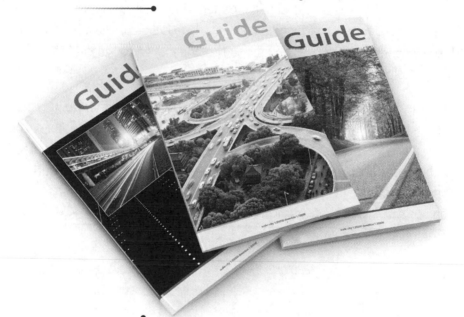

**NIGHT TIME "CATS EYES"**
*(Reflectors in the middle of the road to help with night driving)*

*Opportunities to learn from others who have done something similar outside the company; or who are having great success internally. Learn from these sources, as they can help greatly.*

# Cost

A culture transformation has a considerable cost attached to it, simply because of the volume of people being touched, and the frequency with which they need to be trained. There is the actual cost of the training itself, and the engagement of an organization who can do this training in an effective fashion and a timely manner. There is also the cost of the communication initiatives, and very often ancillary activities such as digital reinforcement, Town Hall meetings, and ongoing management coaching. In addition, there is time off the job in training. Taken together the hard costs and the soft costs are often considerable for wide scale transformation.

However, **the issue should not be one of cost, but one of value**. It is easy to spend money and then evaluate the payback compared to the amount spent. With culture transformation, it is preferable to first evaluate the foreseen impact on the organization and the benefit to be received, as well as the consequences of not having done the transformation, and then the related cost of that. Against that view one can assess the value, in both hard and soft costs, of the transformation initiative.

 *As an example, a transformation of the sales force may appear to be quite costly when evaluated simply against the metric of money and time spent. On the other hand, if a valuation is done of the total volume of new business as a result of a successful transformation, then the revenue from that new business should be so significant that the cost to achieve it will pale by comparison. In this case, the cost of the transformation is not the issue; rather the real issue is achieving the benefit of the transformation. It's then simply a matter of putting together a suitable budget to achieve that benefit.*

I often feel that organizations look first at the cost and make a "go/no go" decision against that, rather than looking at the benefit, and measuring that. The benefit may at times be difficult to quantify, but one which, once achieved, will clearly be a key pillar in the organization's future success. My earlier sales example is easy to quantify, but an all around increased individual initiative would be much harder to quality. Yet, even then, if every individual demonstrated more initiative around improved productivity, which in turn increased by 5% company-wide, then a measure of success can be created.

While cost is definitely an important issue, it should not be the only focal point. **The focus should begin with the benefit to the organization and an attempt made to quantify that benefit**. Once completed, the question then becomes how much can the organization afford to pay in order to achieve that benefit...this then becomes the cost of the transformation.

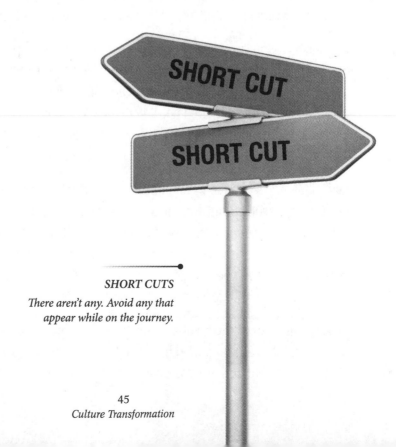

**SHORT CUTS**

*There aren't any. Avoid any that appear while on the journey.*

# The Place for Human Resources

Human Resources plays a vital role in any transformation, but they should not be seen to be the prime driver. The lead drivers of any culture transformation must be senior management. However, Human Resources are their agents.

 The Human Resource function covers off several key components critical to any transformation. The first and most obvious is **training**. For individuals to learn new behaviors they will need new skills and knowledge. They will have to become more competent. Training will do this, and is the purview of Human Resources.

Any transformation will involve a clear focus on **communication**, and this is often housed under Human Resources, or they will have to liaise closely with the Communications group. However, Communications must play a vital role in the overall transformation, and integrating that with Human Resources is important.

The Human Resource generalist function should be there to **support line managers on their journey, assess the effectiveness of the transformation, and give feedback**. The Human Resource generalist is key to keeping track of the transformation's success and impact within the company, and providing objective feedback as to where it is being successful, or which departments or areas need more attention.

Any culture transformation should be linked to **performance management, recruiting, career planning, succession planning, and promotion**. Each of these are individual components of the Human Resource function, and each needs to reflect that success with the adoption of the new behaviors on the part of any individual will be reflected in the way in which they are assessed within the organization, both for performance, and for promotion.

**Reward and recognition** also needs to be linked to the culture transformation, and again, these are supported by Human Resources, who are charged with integrating reward and recognition into the organization's DNA.

Inasmuch as the culture transformation is about human behavior, and how people need to behave differently, it naturally falls under the responsibility of Human Resources, who are responsible for the people side of the business. However, it is often the case that it would be a challenge for the Human Resources group to undertake an initiative of this nature and scope simply because they do not have the background or experience required. This is not to their detriment, it is simply a fact. There are consultants available who specialize in culture transformation, and the related HR practices, and who can be drawn upon to help. When this is the case, then this consulting team should work closely with Human Resources, as well as senior management, to deliver the outcome. It still remains a Human Resources accountability, but essentially the consulting team becomes an arm of Human Resources, working under their banner, but with a defined purpose and scope focused exclusively on the transformation.

When selecting a consultant care must be taken to select one which has the changing of human behavior as a focus. There are a number of consulting firms in the transformation business who are more skilled in the areas of measuring, monitoring, assessing, and tracking. They are able to help an organization identify if a transformation is necessary, and what the transformation should look like, but their area of expertise is not the subsequent execution of that plan. Changing behavior is not an easy task, and specialists in that particular area will add immensely to the success of the transformation.

Often one consulting team will come in and identify the need for the transformation, measure its potential impact and benefit, and help to define what the resulting organization should look like. The mantle then passes to a second team of consultants who are able to actually come in with an experienced facilitation team, and the ability to create the appropriate content in order to ensure that the transformation is successful. They provide training for the leaders and individuals on the new behaviors, and ensure that the training is relevant, powerful, and sustainable.

*WAY POINTS*

*Celebrating success at critical crossroads along the journey with a formal recognition program including positive feedback from leaders, colleagues, and shareholders.*

# Implementation

An organization and its culture is initially like a stable hourglass, with each grain of sand nestled peacefully in the bottom half of the hourglass. A culture transformation turns the hourglass upside down, and the sand must react. Employees affected by a culture transformation are like those grains of sand.

Some – the early adopters – move quickly to the bottom, embrace the change, and move on; others cling to the sides, much slower to move, but ultimately get there. Lastly, some, usually those who believe the transformation affects them least – who feel they're furthest away from it – are the last to participate.

A successful culture transformation seeks to widen the neck of the hourglass as quickly as possible and to as large a degree as possible. Within this context, there are typically three groups which can be identified once a transformation begins.

1.  **The Promoters.** There are always early adopters in any transformation, and these people are huge assets on the journey, as they are always at the forefront at each stage of the transformation, remain its ardent supporters, and are the ones who can be counted on to truly demonstrate the power of the new behaviors. When the promoters are also on the high potentials list that is the ideal situation, as the high potentials are typically seen as the ones against whom others compare themselves.

2.  **The Followers.** These are the second group, and by far make up the largest number of people. These are the ones who adopt the new ways of behaving and make them a part of their day-to-day activity, but over time. Some of the followers will come on board early on, and some later on, depending on their own rate of learning, their degree of understanding, and the quality of their own leader. It is not that they are resistive; it is more simply that they take time to change, and adopt the new ways of thinking.

Followers can become promoters over time, and that would be the goal. For this to happen their own leaders must be enthusiastic in their leading of the new ways of behaving, and in their support of others.

3.  **The Naysayers.** The third and last group are typically a small percentage and represents those who essentially refuse to accept the transformation as the new way of behaving. They resist it either passively or actively, and despite the time given them to adopt the new ways of behaving, may still adamantly refuse to do so. In my judgment a conversation should be had with them that simply explains that this transformation is permanent and is not going away, and that they should decide whether or not they want to be part of this organization in its new form, or not. If not, then they should seek out another organization whose culture is more suited to their own needs and values. If the resistance still persists then I would recommend that these individuals be released from the company.

It is very difficult for groups of individuals trying to adopt a new way of behaving when one or two of their colleagues are clearly seen to be adamantly opposed, aggressively resisting it, and yet still tolerated by management. This sends a confusing message to those who are attempting to apply new behaviors, as they will then begin to question how serious the organization is about their adoption. If after considerable time one or more individuals are clearly seen to be determined to resist the new expectations, then action should be taken which will reinforce for the others that the organization is serious about this transformation, making it work, and receiving the benefits.

*SPEED LIMITS*
*A reminder that culture transformation can't be rushed. It requires a sustained, consistent pace.*

# Beyond the Company's Walls

A relevant question is whether or not a transformation going on within an organization should formally extend outside the walls of the company upstream to suppliers and downstream to customers. Conceptually, I would say absolutely, but clearly it is dependent on the nature of the transformation.

If what is going on within the company can in some way benefit the customer or the supplier, then including them would be appreciated, and it would accelerate what is going on within the organization. If on the other hand the transformation is essentially unique to the organization itself, then neither customer nor supplier will see the value of being included, nor want to be. Judgment needs to be applied in this case, but the consideration of including them should not automatically be ruled out.

In addition, an alternative may be to look at the components of the transformation and realize that some aspects, but perhaps not all, would be of interest or value to customers or suppliers. In this case the offer could be made to the outside parties to determine for themselves whether they would like to be involved in some fashion.

 *For example, innovation training may be a part of the transformation, and the customers and suppliers may feel as though they would benefit, and would therefore welcome the opportunity to be included. On the other hand, some form of internal empowerment may be an aspect of the total transformation, and one clearly that will touch only values and behaviors within the company itself, and so be of little interest to those outside.*

**HIGHLIGHTED ROUTE**

*A clear line of sight between where the organization is now, and where it intends to end up.*

**HISTORIC SITES LOCATED ON THE ROAD**

*Periodic opportunities to pause, assess progress, review the map, and course correct where necessary.*

# Compensation and Performance Management

From a leadership perspective it is possible to measure the behavior of the leaders through a 360° assessment. This essentially provides those for whom the leader is responsible the opportunity to give that leader feedback in terms of the quality of their leadership, and demonstration of key behaviors. This is a powerful feedback tool and one which can be used by the organization to help leaders on their journey towards modeling, coaching, and requiring the behaviors of the new transformation.

It is not essential to link the 360° feedback tool to performance management, but if it is done carefully, and thoughtfully, then it can be. Whether or not this particular approach is taken will depend largely on the culture and experience of the organization; and the previous usage they have made of 360° assessments.

Similarly, the behaviors and values associated with the transformation can be explicitly identified and codified. These can then be included on regular performance management tools used within the organization to link the behaviors to performance, and to give feedback to each individual on the related impact of that performance.

**One of the most impactful ways to improve performance is through feedback.** This is true in every instance, whether in sports, relationships, activities such as writing and music, or corporate behaviors. The individual responsible for the feedback within the corporation should be the line manager, and one of the tools used can be some form of performance appraisal or assessment.

Performance management is also an important tool in the determination of promotion, and succession planning. As such it provides a common and objective way to integrate the selections being made for future leaders in the organization with the culture transformation, and should be used to do so.

In the majority of organizations compensation is linked to performance, and performance is linked to performance management tools. If the culture transformation is a portion of the total performance management package then clearly there will be some link between it and compensation; however, a direct link is not recommended because the culture transformation is not a goal in itself. The goal should not be to compensate the behavior, but rather the results of the behavior. Feedback should be the tool used to shape behavior, compensation the tool used to impact results.

*THE ROAD TO BE FOLLOWED*
*Training provided on the new behaviors.*

# Onboarding and Recruitment

For those joining the organization through recruitment and onboarding there really is no such thing as a culture transformation. They are joining an organization with a defined culture, albeit one in transition; and should immediately adopt the defined cultural norms, even if some are new to those already employed by the organization. Individuals should be hired who demonstrate the kinds of behaviors, attitudes, and approaches which the culture transformation is striving to build within the organization. By recruiting people who reflect the behaviors being taught in the transformation it is possible to accelerate the transformation, and reinforce the organization's commitment to it.

 *This is another example of the importance of linking the transformation to other HR practices. New employees should be selected, among other things, on the basis of their alignment with the new culture, and the subsequent onboarding process should simply be a reinforcement of the new behaviors.*

*If it is not possible to find candidates who fully reflect the new culture, then the onboarding process, and the training associated with it, will align them, along with all the other organizational employees, towards the behaviors required within the company going forward. They will merely be caught up in the larger initiative as they too strive to demonstrate the behaviors expected by the company.*

# Measurement

I think it is difficult to actually measure culture, and I am not sure that it should actually be measured. There are, however, a number of ways in which a culture can be documented, and from that documentation a decision made as to whether or not management is happy with the progress of the transformation, and the culture in general.

Starting first with the issue of measurement, I believe **the true focus should not be the measuring of the culture, but the measuring of the benefit or outcome of the culture**. This is much easier, and far more practical. Shareholders are interested in the value which the organization is providing, and the culture is a component of providing that value. When evaluating a culture the real focus should be on evaluating the impact of that culture. Various transformations will require various ways of assessing the impact as identified below.

1. **Empowerment or Engagement.** This is often the area which organizations wish to tackle most frequently, that is: how best to more effectively engage the workforce, releasing individual potential, and having people take more ownership both for the outcomes, and for the activities which influence those outcomes. A highly engaged workforce has a greater willingness to participate and initiate. Greater engagement means individuals have such a high degree of trust in their company that they will do all the things that need to be done, the way they always need to be done, simply because they know it's right; rather than merely doing what they are told even when they know that there's a better way, or worse, when they know that what they are being told to do is in fact wrong. These are all different outcomes of engagement, and each can be measured depending on which outcome is sought, to what end, and with what result. Once the outcome has been identified then the measurement can be designed to determine whether or not it has occurred.

2.  **Innovation.** Another area where culture transformation is often sought is in the area of innovation. It is important not to confuse innovation with ideation. Ideation is coming up with new ideas or thoughts. It is essentially "blue sky" thinking. Innovation occurs when ideation has first happened, and then a rigorous process is followed in order to bring those ideas to fruition for the benefit of the shareholder. Once the organization has benefited from innovative ideas, then true innovation has occurred. Therefore, the measure of an innovative culture is a measure of how many innovative ideas, thoughts, processes, or activities have been initiated and executed through to the end, so as to add value to the organization.

3.  **Sales.** Often organizations wish is to transform their sales force, either to equip them to deliver a new product or service, to approach a new market, to approach existing markets in a different fashion, or to adopt new tools or ways of behaving. In these cases the measurement is much simpler. The intention behind this type of transformation is clearly to grow sales, and presumably customer loyalty. These things are readily measured, and that would be the measure of the transformation.

4.  **Leadership Excellence.** Organizations at times find themselves lagging behind in terms of the quality of their leadership and wish to transform that leadership into something that could be described as world class. In this case the measures are more difficult. Clearly, some form of 360° assessment is important to determine whether or not leaders are adopting the new behaviors of the transformation, but that is still only measuring activity. To truly measure leadership effectiveness one needs to have a deep-seated conviction that great leaders will produce great results. The quality of any organization's output is directly related to the quality of their leadership. If this conviction is in place, then the measure of great leadership will be the overall performance of the organization.

In this instance, the best place to look for the measures of the transformation is to the measures already in place that measure the overall success of the organization. They could be things such as productivity, turnover, speed to market, working capital, sales per employee ratios, process improvements, waste elimination, etc. Each of these is the direct result of leaders leading people. If the leadership is great then the performance of the people will also be great, and as leadership competency improves, so should overall performance.

*DASHBOARD*

*Ongoing data collected and used to monitor progress, and give input to those charged with the implementation.*

1. *Subjective – employee surveys*
2. *Objective – corporate metrics*

5. **Customer Focus.** This is another area where transformation is often a focus, and the measures here should be twofold. In the first case, asking the customers whether they feel the company is in fact becoming more customer focused and better at meeting their needs is a clear option. However, there's also the area of the results of greater customer focus. This should show in terms of loyalty, repeat business, larger invoice or check size, increased word-of-mouth, and a willingness to form deeper more sustained and long-lasting partnerships. If these things are occurring, and are measured, they will provide a reflection of the effectiveness of the transformation.

In my experience any culture transformation should have the people responsible for implementing the transformation working side-by-side with the office of the CFO. A true transformation is a very expensive initiative to undertake, both in terms of hard and soft costs, and can have very far reaching effects. The CFO is charged with the financial health of the organization, and as such looks at any initiative in terms of its impact, either positive or negative. Given the potential for a culture transformation to have a very significant positive impact on any organization the involvement of the CFO is critical.

The same measures that are being applied to any other initiative within the organization, such as improved sales skills, additional marketing, new factories, additional software or an acquisition, should all apply equally to the culture transformation. If anything, the transformation could have far more significant and wider reaching implications than most other initiatives within the company, so it should have even closer financial scrutiny and support from the beginning.

**Beyond these more objective measurements there is the actual mindset of the employees**. This is essentially a documentation of the culture. In this case, the organization could do periodic pulse checks on how the employees feel about the culture.

The phrase "pulse check" is a very accurate one. In the same way that a doctor checks the health of a patient by checking their pulse, so organizations can check the health of a culture by taking its pulse. Done properly, this is a way in which the culture, and any transformation work, can be captured and codified.

By capturing how people think and feel it is possible to get an accurate reflection of the current culture as viewed by the individuals working there. However, this is not always a foolproof approach, as many things can intervene to skew this data in some way. At times results need to be evaluated within the context of a larger reality. For example, if there is a global recession underway and every employee is feeling the impact of that in some fashion, they will be unable to disassociate that from the culture which they are experiencing within their own company. In fact, their own company's culture may also be temporarily influenced by the recession, and any employee evaluation will reflect this influence. In this case a pulse check may not be evaluating the culture, but the way in which the culture is responding to the circumstances.

Another consideration that can skew the data is that an organization may already have an outstanding culture, which has raised the expectations of the workforce to a very high level, and they are now evaluating their culture against those expectations. In this case, management should certainly pay attention to what the people are saying, but then add their own judgment. It may be, for example, that the employees rate communication as needing attention, but in comparison, the communication within that company is vastly superior to that within many other organizations. This kind of judgment and awareness needs to be taken into account when evaluating employee input.

It is in situations like this where it is valuable to have an outside partner helping with the transformation, and the assessment of it, in order to provide a broader view, and bring their experience to bear.

Once the transformation is underway these pulse checks should continue, as they provide milestones along the journey as well as opportunities to celebrate success and progress. They also flag areas that need pinpointing and focused attention if some aspect of the transformation is not moving ahead as desired.

# Celebrate Success Along the Journey

As the organization moves along the transformation path there will be hurdles to be overcome, challenges to be met, and unforeseen drawbacks, as with any complex initiative. But there will also be successes, high points, and significant milestones crossed. Each of these positive steps towards the final outcome should be acknowledged and celebrated, appropriate to the achievement.

**Success breeds success**. Often clear progress on the longer path to ultimate success is taken for granted, and simply part of the expectations, so there is inadequate focus on recognizing that progress. True, progress should be expected, but it should also be celebrated so those on the journey develop a sense of "we're winning...we're making headway, and that's good!" This sense of succeeding encourages continued effort, and especially so when the transformation encounters a challenging period. A very effective way to celebrate progress is to link recognition of accomplishment to key milestones that had been previously identified as critical.

> *For example, in a transformation around improved quality the first milestone might be being removed from a customer's "get it right or lose the business" list. In a transformation around innovation the first milestone might be having every employee participate in their first Ideation meeting; a second milestone could be when the first innovative idea is approved for implementation; and a third milestone could be when that idea has successfully improved the organization's performance. Each of these provides an opportunity for "celebration."*

**SNACK FOOD**

*Informal reinforcement and sharing of successes by colleagues with one another. Digital tools can facilitate this.*

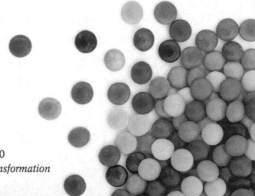

There can be many other instances when celebration of progress is possible... when an individual does something noteworthy, or when a department or function contributes to the new cultural aspirations in some remarkable fashion, or a leader particularly stands out for some aspect of leading the transformation, perhaps through coaching or helping brilliantly with the training.

The key is to know what actions or results would be clearly seen as examples of living the new culture, then finding instances of those within the organization. From there the corporate communication team can make them widely known, and celebrate their effectiveness.

"Celebration" can take many forms. Sometimes what's appropriate is simply recognition at the departmental level by a leader of an employee's progress or success. At other times that recognition can be more widespread, reaching out to a broader audience, usually through a corporate communication vehicle. Celebration can also include recognition by senior management via a short email of thanks, or attending a presentation by a particularly successful team on what they achieved, or even a lunch meeting with a member of the senior team. Using senior management's support in this way can go a long way towards recognizing those who have adopted the behaviors of the culture transformation and are making a difference as a result. It also reinforces for the rest of the organization the importance of each individual adopting the new behaviors.

Whatever the approach, the power and necessity of celebrating progress should not be ignored. It reinforces for the organization what's important, it reiterates management's commitment to the transformation, and it builds a winning spirit. People see that success is not only possible, but actually occurring, and from that realization remain motivated to stay the course.

**Transformation – the learning and application of new behaviors – is as much a matter of the heart and personal conviction as it is knowing what to do**. Celebration of success feeds those emotions. Staying the course feeds the intellect; recognition of progress on the journey feeds the passion.

# Priorities

It is often assumed that any culture transformation needs to be the highest priority within any company. This is not necessarily the case.

In the lifecycle of any organization there are many initiatives underway, usually all happening simultaneously. Senior management needs to have a clear view of all current initiatives, and also of those intended to be initiated shortly. Each of these should have an anticipated and defined impact on the organization, and a foreseen return, either objective or subjective.

 *For example, a major marketing initiative could have as a direct objective achieving improved results on the bottom line; a focus on environmental responsibility could have as a clear mandate improving how the company is perceived by its consumers.*

It is usually within this vast swirling sea of priorities that culture transformation is introduced. Along with all the other things underway, both short-term and long-term, senior management has decided that the organization would benefit from a culture transformation and is taking steps accordingly. Once this decision is made then the relative priority of implementing that culture transformation should be assessed within the context of all the other priorities.

Sometimes the culture transformation will be very high on the priority list because it is seen to be something urgently and critically needed and which will have widespread benefits to virtually all other initiatives underway. Sometimes the culture transformation will be more narrow in scope, and be felt to be simply another important issue to be dealt with. Whatever the judgment, **the relative priority of the culture transformation should be clearly established, and then communicated**.

The most important thing is to understand that, once begun, the culture transformation needs to be carried through to completion. Whatever its priority, it still must be executed flawlessly. Its ranking in terms of priority will determine issues such as how quickly the transformation needs to occur, how many resources will be allocated to it, and how much time leaders within the company are expected to spend on it. However, whatever the priority decided upon, it must then be made clear to all concerned, and sustained.

*DISTRACTIONS*
*Stay on course. Avoid getting*
*sidetracked for any reason.*

DON'T MISS COMING HERE...

YOU MUST SEE THIS!

THE ONE AND ONLY!

# Painful or Exciting?

The common folklore is that creating a new culture will probably be painful in some fashion; either it will require people to do things which they do not want to do, or take too much time that they don't have, or be something which is felt to perhaps be important but actually not urgent. By no means should this be the case, nor does it need to be the case.

Quite the contrary, **a culture transformation can be a very exciting time that harnesses the energy and enthusiasm of the entire workforce**. Training should be exciting and engaging, not death by PowerPoint. Learning should be done in a way that requires people to think and discuss, evaluate, consider and form opinions, not simply be lectured at. Transformation should be seen as something moving the company into an exciting future, that will give it a competitive advantage or address a significant problem, or in some way accelerate the other great benefits of the organization.

This is not simply window-dressing or sugarcoating the situation, it is the situation. Any culture transformation is an opportunity to fully engage the workforce in an exciting time. It is an opportunity to provide them with skills that can last a lifetime.

A true culture transformation that is well implemented captures hearts and minds, as well as hands. It is seen as something that people are excited about and willing to support. When it is done properly, and seen to be led by management, then the organization will be quick to support it and eager to reap the benefits.

This is not to say that learning new behaviors is easy, or that existing ways of doing things are not deeply engrained and well entrenched. They are. However, changing these existing behaviors to new ways of doing things does not have to be painful; it can breathe new life into a workforce if done well.

It is important to remember that individuals within the company are giving their all, and doing their best at any point in time. If it is felt that more is possible, and other ways of doing things would be preferable, then shifting that will require effort, probably some consternation, maybe some confusion, and at times some frustration; but this is normal, and true for any initiative. However, this does not have to be disconcerting, it merely has to be recognized, accommodated for, and overcome with a transformation plan that is well designed and implemented.

"A true culture transformation should outlast the management that initiated it."

Phil Geldart

**BILLBOARDS**

*Visual reminders, electronic and/or on posters, of the new behaviors to be implemented.*

# When to Start

It's remarkable the number of times people have indicated that they feel a culture transformation needs to be made, is vital, and critical, but: "We have to wait for something to be done first," or "We're not quite ready," or the organization has to achieve something before the culture transformation begins, such as a structural change, a product launch, or completion of some other initiative.

I would suggest that since a culture is the sum total of the behaviors demonstrated by the employees there's already a clear culture within the organization, and that culture is currently being applied to whatever the present reality is within the company.

That is to say that the things currently underway, which "need to be finished before the transformation" are in fact already being significantly influenced by the existing culture. If it is felt that the existing culture needs to be transformed in some way then I would suggest that there's not a moment to lose. Begin the transformation immediately, so that all other initiatives reap the benefit.

It might be argued that the organization cannot handle that much change, or that people are already overworked, or that somehow things will ease up once some other initiative has been completed. In my experience this is rarely the case. There are always things underway, or that have to be re-prioritized. The culture is merely a reflection of the way people do things. If the transformation is going to change the way people do things, and this change is for the better, then the sooner they can learn and apply these things the greater will be the impact. It is simply a matter of bearing in mind all the other priorities and urgencies with which the organization is coping so that the introduction of the new behaviors is seen to be seamless, complementary, and helpful.

**The time for the transformation is when it is recognized that the transformation is needed.**

# The Finish Line

**A transformation does come to an end**. Once the new behaviors have been trained, and adopted by the employees of the organization, and the benefit seen, then the transformation work is complete.

At this point the organization will have a new culture. It may be widespread if that was the objective, or focused within a particular division or function; but one way or another the organization will be reflective of the new behaviors that have been trained, modelled, coached, and required over the recent years. The transformation has occurred.

**The next step is to sustain that new culture**.

This is not a reflection of a poor job in implementing the culture. It is merely recognizing that human nature is such that the things that are important need to be kept top of mind. As new things happen within the company, such as new products, an acquisition or divestiture, new leadership, or competitive pressure, the employees of the organization will need to continually be reminded how the culture should dictate how they behave under those circumstances. This is not unique to a culture transformation, it is simply sound management practices for any culture.

Any organization's culture needs to constantly receive attention and focus as the world around the employees shifts, moves, and mutates. Keeping the culture alive is an important responsibility of leadership, and it does not end simply because a lot of work has gone in to creating a new culture. The new culture is now the culture, and as such needs to be sustained with intentionality and focus.

# A Great Culture

Organizations have unique cultures, and I think it's important to understand that "one size does not fit all." As I mentioned earlier, there are some organizations where a great culture will be defined in terms of hours worked and revenue brought in, such as in a company where billings are paramount. Another company will define culture in terms of impact on people's lives and communities, such as an organization committed to poverty relief.

**Each organization needs its own culture. This culture should be a reflection of what is important to them, and what is necessary for them to succeed in their marketplace**. There's no such thing, in my opinion, as a single great culture. What makes a culture truly great is whether or not it optimizes the talent and ability of the people. Each individual can select which organization they choose to work for based on the culture they wish to be part of. Once there, then they should acknowledge that the culture should be such that it optimizes the value which that organization provides to its consumers, shareholders, and constituents. The culture is a vehicle for doing this, and the better it does that, the better the culture. The individual's accountability is then to support that culture.

In the course of doing business senior management may feel that they have not optimized the potential and willingness of the organization, or the talent and skill of the people, or provided what is necessary for optimum success going forward. In each of these cases a culture transformation is required, but this transformation is to move from what is, to what is preferred.

I would add, though, that often an organization may not be aware of what could be, and therefore may feel as though they do in fact have a great culture, or that they truly know what a great culture looks like. However, they may not have a broad enough understanding to make that judgment as accurately as they could with a greater view of what was possible.

This is simply a caution to ensure that we do not become complacent in the evaluation of our culture. We need to understand what is possible, what others are doing, and what can be, before we make the final decision as to whether or not our culture is in fact truly great, or if some form of culture transformation would make us even greater.

# YOUR OWN PATH FORWARD

## Personal Workshop

The following section provides a
"Personal Workshop."
Reflecting on, and then answering these
key questions will move you well
along the path to putting a plan in place for your
own culture transformation.

## Start

*Initial discovery: What defines our culture now? How would our people describe it?*

1.  What defines our culture now, with respect to the desired transformation?

2.  What words would our people use to describe our culture, in those areas that would be affected by the transformation?

## End

*After the transformation: How will we be described? What will be the outcome, benefit, or impact?*

1.  What words would we like to be used to describe our culture after the transformation?

2.  What will improve, or be different as a result of the transformation?

## The Map of the Route

*The plan for the transformation. Usually created by HR and/or outside consultants, and approved by senior management.*

1. Who will be ultimately accountable for the tactical side of implementing the transformation?

2. What resources (people, budget) will be made available in support?

3. Should an experienced outside company be involved?

---

## Highlighted Route

*A clear line of sight between where the organization is now, and where it intends to end up.*

1. To maintain the line of sight, what can be done by:
   - Senior management?
   - Line management?
   - The communications team?

## GPS

*Senior management's visible support and leadership of the transformation.*

1. How can senior management best demonstrate their support for:
   - The transformation?
   - The adoption of the new behaviors?

---

## The Driver

*Each individual within the organization.*

1. For a company-wide transformation – is there any reason not to include everyone?

2. For a subset of the company:
   - Who will be included?
   - Are there any support areas which should also be included?

## The Car

*The way work is being done every day.*

1. What behaviors are currently in evidence before the transformation?

2. As a result of the transformation, what behaviors should be:
   - Stopped?
   - Started?
   - Continued?

———————————

## Other Occupants

*Immediate supervisor (line manager), mentors, transformation support staff, colleagues.*

1. Other than these listed, are there any other groups that should be included?

## Dashboard

*Ongoing data collected and used to monitor progress, and give input to those charged with the implementation. Subjective – employee surveys; Objective – corporate metrics*

1. What metrics will make up the dashboard?

   Subjective: e.g., Employee surveys, 360° feedback

   Objective: e.g., Existing performance measures

---

## Night Time "Cat's Eyes"

*(Reflectors in the middle of the road to help with night driving). Opportunities to learn from others who have done something similar outside the company; or who are having great success internally. Learn from these sources, as they can help greatly.*

1. What can be done to facilitate this?

## Mile Markers

*Previously identified metrics used as key indicators of progress and crucial to achieve.*

1. Which specific metrics (from the dashboard) should stand out as key indicators of progress, and when should they be reviewed?

---

## The Road to be Followed

*Training provided on the new behaviors.*

1. What words would be used to describe the ideal training solution?

2. Will company leaders be willing to "team teach" some of the content? Are there any related constraints?

## In-Car Entertainment

*An intentional focus on ensuring the transformation journey remains engaging and positive.*

1.  What are some suggestions for keeping what will be a multi-year initiative top of mind, and engaging?

## Gas

*Ongoing communication that maintains a "line of sight" to the destination, and reinforces the rationale for the transformation.*

1.  Who will be responsible for all related communication?

2.  What contributions can senior management make to the content of the communication?

## Speed Limits

*A reminder that culture transformation can't be rushed. It requires a sustained, consistent pace.*

1.  How can this message best be reinforced, and followed, during the transformation?

## Mountain Passes

*Some aspects of the transformation will be much harder (uphill going!) than others (downhill going!). Stay the course, it's simply part of the journey.*

1.  Where do you anticipate some challenging uphill, slower going?

2.  Where do you think the transformation will be comparatively easy?

## Snack Food

*Informal reinforcement and sharing of successes by colleagues with one another. Digital tools can facilitate this.*

1. What can be put in place to encourage colleagues to share successes internally?

2. Who should be accountable for making this happen?

## Distractions

*Stay on course. Avoid getting sidetracked for any reason.*

1. What could take attention away from this initiative to such a degree as to sidetrack it?

2. How can these be avoided?

## Slower Cars

*Be patient. Not everyone will learn and adapt at the same pace.*

1. What can you do to bring an appreciation of this fact to the "faster" cars?

## Rearview Mirror

*Competitive activity in the marketplace.*

1. How could competitive information be used to reinforce the rationale for the transformation?

2. What would be some suggested ways to present this information in an impactful and relevant way?

## Waypoints

*Celebrating success at critical crossroads along the journey with a formal recognition program including positive feedback from leaders, colleagues, and shareholders.*

1. What are the critical junctures foreseen, the crossing of which should be celebrated?

2. What would be the most appropriate way to celebrate at each juncture?

## Car Maintenance

*Leader led reinforcement activities done periodically by each leader with their own teams.*

1. How frequently should line managers be asked to run reinforcement workshops with their direct reports?

2. How long should each workshop be?

3. Should there be pre and/or post work required in support of these short workshops?

## Rainstorms

*A period when there are many competing priorities co-existing with the transformation.*

1. What other priorities might compete with the culture transformation for time and attention?

2. How can you help the organization stay appropriately balanced?

## Short Cuts

*There aren't any. Avoid any that appear while on the journey.*

1. What might happen that could look like an enticing shortcut, but which should still be avoided?

## Hurdles

*Some hurdles may appear which could block progress. Identify the hurdle and quickly find a response to sustain the focus on the transformation.*

1. What are some likely hurdles you may encounter?

2. What would be a practical response to them?

---

## City Driving

*Times when the requirements of the business (e.g., year end) simply slow everything down, including the transformation activities.*

1. What could constitute "passing through a city" for you?

## Country Driving

*Times when nothing stands in the way of accelerating the culture transformation activities.*

No action required!

## Historic Sites Located on the Road

*Periodic opportunities to pause, assess progress, review the map, and course correct where necessary.*

1. Where is it most appropriate to pause, reassess, and course correct if necessary?

2. What would be observed there to indicate:

   - No substantial changes necessary?

   - Significant changes required?

## Fog Everywhere

*The vision for the transformation seems lost, or unfocussed. Engage senior management ("the GPS") to quickly move back into a place of clarity and purpose.*

1. What will be the observable signs that you've entered some "fog"?

2. What actions should senior management take at these times?

## Billboards

*Visual reminders, electronic and/or on posters, of the new behaviors to be implemented.*

1. How prevalent should these be?

2. What form should they take?

3. What should be their content?

# Closing

Eagle's Flight is a recognized expert in truly transforming culture, and working closely with companies to ensure their success in this challenging area.

For more information, or to arrange to speak with Phil, please contact Eagle's Flight at:

**www.eaglesflight.com**
International Phone: 1-519-767-1747
Canada and USA: 1-800-567-8079

# Other Books by Phil Geldart

**IN YOUR HANDS**
The Behaviors of a
World-Class Leader

**LEAD YOURSELF,
LEAD OTHERS**
Eight Principles of
Leadership

**THE SEVEN
CORNERSTONES
OF TEAMWORK**

**THE LEADER'S
TRIAD**
The Power of Clarity,
Team and the Individual

**IN SEARCH OF
THE GOLD OF THE
DESERT KINGS**
A Journey of My Travels